FAN *into* FLAME

EMBRACE GOD'S PURPOSE, DISCOVER GOD'S PROVISIONS

SANDRA JACKSON

Copyright © 2024 Sandra Jackson
Scripture quotations marked (KJV) are taken from the King James Version, public domain. Scripture quotations marked (Amp) are taken from the Amplified® Bible, Copyright© 1954, 1958, 1962, 1964, 1965, 1987 by the Lockman Foundation Used by Permission. (www.Lockman. org). Scripture quotations marked (ESV) are taken from The Holy Bible, English Standard Version®, Copyright© 2001 by Crossway, a publishing ministry of Good News Publishers. Used by permission. Scripture quotations marked (TLB) are taken from The Living Bible copyright © 1971. Used by permission of Tyndale House Publishers, Carol Stream, Illinois 60188. All rights reserved. Scripture quotations marked MSG are taken from The Message, copyright © 1993, 2002, 2018 by Eugene H. Peterson. Used by permission of NavPress, represented by Tyndale House Publishers. All rights reserved. Scripture quotations marked (NASB) are taken from the New American Standard Bible®, Copyright© 1960, 1962, 1963, 1968, 1971, 1972, 1973, 1975, 1977, 1995 by The Lockman Foundation. Used by permission. Scripture quotations marked (NET) are taken from the Net Bible® copyright ©1996-2006 by Biblical Studies Press, L.L.C. http://netbible. com All rights reserved. The names: The Net Bible®, New English Translation Copyright © 1996 By Biblical Studies Press, L.l.c. Net Bible® is a registered trademark The Net Bible® Logo, Service Mark Copyright © 1997 By Biblical Studies Press, L.l.c. All Rights Reserved. Scripture quotations marked (NIV) are taken from The Holy Bible, New International Version®. Copyright© 1973, 1978, 1984, 2011 by Biblica, Inc.™. Used by permission of Zondervan. Scripture quotations marked (NKJV) are taken from the New King James Version®. Copyright© 1982 by Thomas Nelson, Inc. Used by permission. All rights reserved. Scripture quotations marked TPT are from The Passion Translation®. Copyright © 2017, 2018, 2020 by Passion & Fire Ministries, Inc. Used by permission. All rights reserved. ThePassionTranslation.com. No part of this document may be reproduced or transmitted in any form or by any means, electronic, mechanical, photocopying, recording, or otherwise, without prior written permission of the author.

FAN INTO FLAME
Embrace God's Purpose, Discover God's Provisions

Sandra Jackson
sjoyj@sbcglobal.net

ISBN 978-1-949826-72-2

Printed in the USA.

All rights reserved
Published by: EAGLES GLOBAL BOOKS | Frisco, Texas
In conjunction with the 2024 Eagles Authors Course
Cover & interior designed by DestinedToPublish.com

"For this reason I remind you to fan into flame the gift of God, which is in you through the laying on of my hands."
(2 Timothy 1:6 NIV)

FOREWORD

I pastored a multiracial church that became the flagship congregation for an evangelical, formally all-white denomination. This church was awarded the title of Chicago's Outstanding Church of the Year by the Greater Sunday School Association of Chicago. I co-authored a book, Breaking Down Walls, that earned the Gold Medallion Book Award. That book was based on the racial reconciliation experiences in the church. These achievements were due in large part to the dance ministry described in this book. I was captivated by the dance ministry and always had complete trust that it would honor God and bless the members of our church.

Choreography, attire, movement, and song selection are individually and collectively capable of sending the wrong message to an audience. Consequently, each one of those elements must meet the standards of being appropriate and God-honoring. Every presentation of Sandra's dance worship rendered a perfection of God-honoring worship without exception. An epic presentation occurred at the National Annual Conference of our conservative evangelical denomination. I was selected to be a keynote speaker, and my gospel choir was selected to render two songs. Dance was not permitted or practiced in that denomination. I decided to do one song by my choir and one presentation by my dance ministry. My book, message, song, and dance ministry were all designed to communicate the message of reconciliation. My choir was racially mixed. The dance team comprised four members: African American, Asian, white, and Latino. They danced to Steve Green's rendition of "Let the Walls Come Down." I placed my reputation, which was sterling, at risk within the denomination where I had spoken in at least 100 churches. The result was a standing ovation that lasted at least five minutes. My reputation went through the roof. Why? The God-honoring professional acumen of Sandra Jackson.

READ THIS BOOK AND YOU WILL UNDERSTAND HOW AND WHY THIS DANCE MINISTRY WAS FANNED INTO FLAMES!

Doctor Raleigh B. Washington
President/CEO of Awakening the Voice of Truth
Pastor Emeritus, Rock Church

President Emeritus, Promise Keepers

Since the beginning, Sandra has integrated her gifts and calling to the purposes of the Kingdom of God; her honesty and sincerity are evident as she bares her soul and insight in this book. As she shares about her journey in worship, and true relationship with the Master Creator and Artist, I pray it will inspire readers to greater levels of intimacy with the Master of the heavens and earth.

Pastor Rosalyn Acevedo
River of Life Worship Intl.
Divine Expressions Christian Academy of Worship Arts

ACKNOWLEDGMENTS

To my Heavenly Father: Thank you, God, for giving me guidance, strength, peace, and perseverance throughout this writing journey.

To my family: Thank you for your patience and support throughout this writing adventure.

To Dr. Raleigh B. Washington: Thank you for establishing the foundation that sprouted my spiritual growth and an opportunity to use my gifts in the ministry of movement.

To Pastor Rosalyn Acevedo: Thank you for allowing me to co-labor in ministry with you and contributing to my biblical understanding of the ministry of movement.

To Dr. Pamela Scott: Thank you for providing a platform on which I have acquired a deeper biblical understanding that has impacted my life and my ministry in movement.

To Dr. Dorothy Bounds: Thank you for opening doors that led to new opportunities to exercise my natural and spiritual gifts.

To Pastor Robert Stevenson: Thank you for being an example to Rock Church and the Austin Community in your dedication to preaching and loving God's people.

To all those who graciously supported me in my writing: Thank you for your prayers, contributions, and encouragement.

DEDICATION

I dedicate this book to my Heavenly Father, whom I love, honor, and praise. You are why I wrote this book. I have had the privilege of reflecting on your goodness in my life, and learning more about you in the process.

I dedicate this book to my dear mom, who passed away on July 29, 2022. She would have been immensely proud of my new accomplishment.

I dedicate this book to believers seeking to understand their earthly purpose. God has birthed something in you. Let's put it into action.

CONTENTS

Introduction 1

Chapter 1
Testimony: Discovering My God-Given Purpose 5

Chapter 2
Created for God's Purpose 25

Chapter 3
Gifted for God's Purpose 33

Chapter 4
Overflowing with God's Gifts 47

Chapter 5
Feeding the Flame: Running with God's Gifts 63

A Final Word 77

Appendix 81

INTRODUCTION

While the song played, the dancers made figure-eight movements about the stage. You could see the fluidity of their light blue, angelic-like garments flaring out like the opening of an umbrella as they made numerous chaine turns with motions of splendor and beauty. As the song repeated the line, "The wait is over, walk into your season,"[1] each dancer, one by one, began to walk through a veil represented by two long, white, sheer flags held up like curtains. After walking through the veil, each dancer spontaneously danced down the aisle without holding back their expressions of freedom. As this took place, you could hear an uproar of praise from the audience shouting, "Amen!" Praise the Lord!" and "Hallelujah!" When the song ended, some dancers were walking about and praising God with their hands lifted high and with tears of joy. Other dancers were shouting, "Thank you Jesus!" and "Hallelujah!"

This event at Dorolyn Academy of Music was not just a dance graduation, but a profound spiritual experience. The music, singing, dancing, and other acts of praise and worship created an atmosphere for God's presence. The program included a time of collective praise and worship through singing and dancing. It featured diverse dance presentations by children, teenagers, and adults, showcasing various styles such as hip-hop, ballet, mime, solo dancing, tambourine, and congregational dancing. The event culminated in an uplifting message from a guest speaker and a powerful time of impartation, where each graduating student received individual prayers from the dance teachers and ministers present.

At Dorolyn's dance graduation, students were either discovering, developing, or enhancing their gifts in the dance. As these students found kingdom purpose, the audience was able to partake in God's work. For the non-churchgoers in the audience, that graduation may have been the first time they realized they were seeing, hearing, and experiencing God. For the Christians in the audience, that graduation may have been the encouragement needed to strengthen their faith. For non-believers, that graduation could have planted the seed for them accepting Christ into their hearts. Because students were pursuing and using their gifts, God was able to use that time to touch lives and minister to the people in attendance.

Whether we are ministers of movement, worship leaders, deacons, preachers, doctors, moms, students, husbands, or actors, or whether we have other roles, we are God's gift to the earth. God has called us, as Christians, to help meet the world's needs for the cause of Christ. God has given each of us the hands, feet, mouth, heart, and mind of Jesus to continue the work that Jesus began in proclaiming God's truth and strengthening and unifying the body of Christ. God has given us gifts, talents, and abilities to fulfill His purposes, ultimately glorifying Him. There is a scripture that says, *"Whatever you do, work heartily, as for the Lord and not for men, knowing that from the Lord you will receive the inheritance as your reward. You are serving the Lord Christ"* (Colossians 3:23-24 ESV). God sees us, knows us, and, most importantly, uniquely designed us for His purposes. God is looking for us not to be spectators but to be participators in His kingdom. God wants us to be the "salt of the earth" and "light of the world" as we serve in His kingdom. Do you know the purpose for which God has created you? Do you know why God has given you certain gifts, talents, and abilities? What have you done with the gifts, talents, and abilities God has given you?

This book is a testament to seeing God's provisions when we walk into our purpose. I share my journey from receiving God as my Lord and Savior to being an instrument of His will. With a ministry spanning over 30 years, I bring to you my personal testimonies and experiences, shedding light on the profound topics of God's purposes, callings, and gifts. I've witnessed God's goodness and divine intervention, and I'm fervent about encouraging fellow Christians to use God's gifts in alignment with His divine purpose.

May this book inspire you to answer the call and activate the gifts God has given you effectively. My desire is to see you walk into God's purpose for your life with excellence. In this season, may God empower you with renewed hope as you acquire knowledge that will help you understand your purpose and ignite you to use your gifts. At the end of each chapter, you will find questions to consider as you reflect and make applications. May this journey encourage you to be the person God has called you to be, to reach the people God has called you to reach, and to go to the places where God has called you to go. May you follow God's path and live out your purpose with an abundant life, impacting lives for His glory. One day, we want to hear God say, "Well done, good and faithful servant."

CHAPTER 1

TESTIMONY: DISCOVERING MY GOD-GIVEN PURPOSE

MY PASSION

During my childhood, I was highly active, playful, and inquisitive. I grew up in a single-parent household with my mom, two brothers, and two sisters. Each of my siblings had different interests and endeavors. For myself, I loved playing sports, and I also enjoyed the arts. The arts helped me to escape into a world of positivity, joyfulness, and freedom. I found pleasure in singing, playing the violin at my school, writing songs, drawing, and dancing. More than anything else, I was drawn to singing and dancing.

From childhood through my teenage years, I sang and danced, and dancing became my joy and passion. It was one of the activities that I felt confident in doing. I kept abreast of all the latest dance trends. I danced at home, I danced at house parties, I danced in a high school club, and I danced in a youth talent show. I not only enjoyed secular dancing, but was interested in pursuing all genres of dance. My dream was to be like Debbie Allen and pursue dance in the performing arts.

MY PURSUITS

At the age of 16, I worked a summer job and paid for my first ballet class at Malcolm X College in Chicago. I had no experience with ballet other than what I saw on television. After the first day of attending the ballet class, I began to question my ability as a dancer. I thought I could be like Debbie Allen, but I realized that I did not have enough experience, skill, knowledge, or exposure to dance in the performing arts. At that time, I did not know ballet terminologies like jeté or tondu, nor was I able to achieve the movements correctly. I did not know how intense a dance class could be until I took my first ballet class at Malcolm X. In my discouragement, I dropped the class and returned to the familiar, which was secular dancing. Surprisingly, I was able to find another pathway to the performing arts by joining a marching band called the O'Quinn Royal Gladiators Drum and Bugle Corps. In the band, I learned how to twirl a rifle and a flag. Marching in a band was an exciting but brief experience for me because the parades only happened during the summer, and I participated for only one summer.

After graduating from high school, I decided to attend the University of Illinois in Champaign-Urbana, where I made another attempt at taking dance classes. I was not a dance major, but I took dance classes every semester, including ballet, jazz, and modern dance. Yes, I attempted ballet once again. I was determined to continue to pursue my interest in dancing. I also joined an African dance company called the Omnimov Dance Company. Looking at my college transcript, my dean could not determine if I was a mechanical engineering major or a dance major because I continued to take dance classes. My dean also encouraged it as an outlet for studying.

I signed up for a work-study program during my sophomore year of college to help pay for my college expenses. I was assigned a job as a server working in the cafeteria of my dorm during the breakfast shift. Every morning as I served food, I was captivated by this one student as he went through the food line. This student was not like the other college students who often looked grumpy, half asleep, and speechless while passing through the food line in the morning. Instead, he was always cheerful, always smiling, and always saying "Good morning" every single day. I could not understand at that time why he was always so happy and pleasant. I was not trying to pursue a relationship with him, but I was simply attracted by the uniqueness of his character. He just did not fit into the norm of what would be considered a typical college student at U of I at that time. In my curiosity, I wanted to know why this student was so different.

One day, I decided to approach this student, who I learned was named Michael, and ask him why he was always so happy. Michael told me that he had received Jesus Christ into his life. (Special note: When we receive Christ in our lives, God's glory flows through us. The glory will manifest in each believer differently.) Michael asked me if I was interested in learning about Jesus, and when I complied, he connected me with a female student, who shared more details about who Jesus was. Through that student, I came to accept Jesus Christ into my life. Because of God's glory reflected through Michael, I came to know the Lord. (Special note: The Word says, *"So all of us who have had that veil removed can see and reflect the glory of the Lord. And the Lord—who is the Spirit—makes us more and more like him as we are changed into his glorious image"* [2 Corinthians 3:18 NLT]).

From that point on, my life was transformed. (Special note: The Holy Spirit is doing the work of transforming us into the image of Christ, who is the image of God.) I connected with the Christian organization that Michael was part of called the Navigators, and I joined their Bible study. As time progressed, I was no longer investing so much time in attending parties, nor feeling the pressure from family to pledge to the Zeta sorority. In fact, after three weeks of pledging, I decided to stop pledging, or "drop off line," as they would say. My focus was all about graduating. I continued taking dance classes, but most of my time was dedicated to my studies. By the grace of God, and it was undoubtedly God's grace, I graduated with a degree in mechanical engineering from U of I.

Meeting Michael made a difference in my life because he introduced me to the greatest gift of all, Jesus Christ. It was through Jesus that I was able to graduate as a Black female in the field of mechanical engineering. Michael allowed God's light to shine through him on a college campus, which significantly impacted my life. (Special note: We are to share the good news of Jesus Christ with others. We are to be living examples of God's love. We are to make disciples. We are to reflect God's glory everywhere we go.)

MY PURPOSE

Accepting the Call

In my last semester before graduating, I interned at Control Data Corporation in Minnesota. Because of the very dry, cold weather there, I decided to return to Chicago after graduating from U of I. Desiring to continue my walk with the Lord, I joined a church called Rock of Our Salvation Evangelical Free Church (aka Rock Church), located on the west side of Chicago, where the pastor and founder was Pastor Raleigh B. Washington. During my first few years at Rock Church, I was a "jack of all trades, master of none." I sang in the choir. I was part of the singing ensemble that traveled with my pastor when he spoke at different churches. I served as a youth leader, I was part of the singles ministry, I was part of a fellowship group, and I was part of a discipleship Bible class. After work, I was involved with church activities every day of the week. This was great for a while because all the experiences contributed to my spiritual growth.

Even with my busy schedule, I was still able to take a class at a dance studio now and then. As my faith grew, I began to question whether I should be doing secular or any other type of dancing. Although I had invested so much of my life in dancing, I was ready to give it all up to live for God. When I told my worship leader about my intentions to end my pursuit of dancing, he said to me, "My sister, you don't have to stop dancing, you just need to change partners."

That day, I received a word from the Lord through my worship leader. Although I was willing to make the sacrifice, it was a relief to know that I did not have to follow through with it. God was speaking through my worship leader to let me know that I did not have to stop dancing, I just had to start dancing for Him. I had no clue what that entailed, but I was ready to take the dance in a new direction. I was ready to accept the call to dance for the Lord.

When I started dancing for the Lord, it was a very humbling experience. I did not know what my next steps would or should be. I did not know how to dance in a way that would be pleasing to God. I did not know what type of worship songs to dance to. I did not know what type of dance garments to wear. I could not consult with anyone, because I did not know of anyone else who danced for the Lord. I could only look to God and the question that resonated with me the most was "How do I dance for you, Lord?"

How Do I Dance for You, Lord?

I know you have heard the saying, "God uses ordinary people to do extraordinary things." Well, that became my story. When I started dancing for the Lord, my life began to come full circle. All I could hear God saying to me was "Come as you are." I started as a soloist ministering in a black leotard and African wrap material. It was a relief to learn that I did not have to fake it to make it, but I was able to be accepted by my church regardless of what I wore or what I knew about dance.

While I sought other dance attire to wear, I also had to address the concern that I did not know how to dance for God. Even with my dance background, I was still bewildered by the question of how to move in a way that would be honoring to the Lord. The only person who could help me was God. A verse in Revelation 3 became very real for me during that time. It says, *"Behold, I stand at the door and knock. If anyone hears My voice and opens the door, I will come in to him and dine with him, and he with Me"* (Revelation 3:20 NKJV). This verse is Jesus speaking through the Apostle John, challenging the church at Sardis to get their hearts right. They were neither hot nor cold but lukewarm in their faith, and Jesus was standing at the door of their heart to enter if they let Him in. That verse let me know that I was not alone in this new venture of living by faith and serving Him. God was there for me amid my lack, awkwardness, and uncertainty. I just needed to seek Him, and He would be the one to come in and do the transforming within me.

I began to seek God on how to dance for Him. The first song I ministered to was "What a Mighty God We Serve." As I practiced movements to the song, I learned that my time of practice was about coming before Him with my offering of praise and worship. I then looked at my time of practice as a time of dancing in His presence, before His throne. As I began to look at dance differently, movements became easier and more fluid. I was lifting my hands and moving my feet to express forms of praise as the song and Holy Spirit would lead me. God was crucifying my flesh. I no longer wanted to dance just for entertainment or to move my body. Now, movement was motivated from a heart of worship and about giving praise and honor to God through my body.

Surrendering All

When I started dancing for God, I began to realize that this was not just a ministry but a calling. God had called me to the dance and given me purpose in ministry; now I stood at the feet of His grace to guide me. In the initial stages of my calling, I only knew two scriptures about dance, Psalm 149:3 and Psalm 150:4. With a limited biblical understanding of the dance, I struggled to drown out all the secular music that resonated within my spirit and overpowered my thoughts. I was in a position where I had to depend on God to deliver me. Not only did I need to depend on God's guidance and direction, but I also needed to surrender to God. Surrender is about completely giving up our own will so that we can subject our thoughts, ideas, and deeds to the will and teachings of the Father.[2] I needed to surrender my will so that God could do His will in and through me. If I led the dance ministry according to my will, it would have been more of a performance rather than an actual ministry. I needed to surrender the type of music that I listened to and spend more time listening to the music that would glorify God in the dance. I realized that music significantly impacted my thoughts, attitude, and motives. When I listened to secular music, my flesh reverted to the old way of dancing and thinking. I enjoyed secular music, but to be dedicated to my calling, I had to stop spending so much time listening to it so that I could operate by faith and in God's power in carrying out my role as a minister of dance. I also had to surrender the way I choreographed dances. Everything I needed—the right perspective, the vision, the wisdom, the discernment—all had to come from God because I truly had little to offer apart from Him.

When we lead a ministry, we are not an entity. We are co-laboring with God, with the ministry team, and with church leadership. In my role as the leader of the dance ministry at my church, I was under the submission of God, but I was also under the submission of my pastor. Submission is about yielding to the authority of others out of reverence for God. I needed to submit to my pastor and walk in obedience. As I shared my ideas about dance ministry with him, there were times when Pastor Washington told me to wait. One example was when I wanted the dance ministry to do congregational dancing during praise and worship singing, meaning that while the praise team sang, the dancers would dance. My pastor told me that the church was not ready for that, so it would have to be brought in methodically. Even though dance was the missing third cord in our time of praise and worship, with the singers and musicians being the first and second cords, I had to trust my pastor's judgment. He knew the heart of the church. It took about two to three years before dance was incorporated during the time of praise and worship.

Leading the dance ministry also involved making sacrifices: sacrificing time to study God's Word, time to pray for the ministry and each member of the ministry, time to listen to the ministry song, time to choreograph, and time to prepare to minister (practicing the choreography, delivering devotionals, selecting dance attire, and praying together as a team). As God gave me vision, I always had a verse to support every dance piece that was created. I also had to sacrifice relationships so that I could be surrounded by people who wanted to live for God. This meant spending less time with people who discouraged my spiritual growth and more time with people who encouraged it.

From the time I started dancing for the Lord to the place where I am now, God has been faithful. God was faithful in leading me, providing for me, teaching me, and strengthening me. God's faithfulness has helped me to walk in faith through my journey in the dance ministry. Even when I did not expect it, God used someone to provide me with my first dance garment. After I saw how dance ministers dress, I started designing some of the garments for the dance ministry. I did not have to worry about anything in ministry of movement, because God was making all the provisions.

Serving Through the Dance

As God worked in my life, I developed a heart to start a children's dance ministry. As it progressed, adults became interested in joining the dance ministry. Eventually, I worked with both a children's dance ministry and one for adults. As the children got older, I started a teenage dance ministry and continued to work with the adults.

It was God who was drawing people to the ministry. As I trusted God, He started depositing spiritual gifts within me. The spiritual gifts of teaching, mercy, giving, service, administration, and leadership became more evident. God guided me in how to lead a ministry. I had to stay before the Lord because my endeavors were rooted in a covenant relationship with Him in which God fulfills all His promises to me. In 2 Chronicles 6:14, it says, *"O LORD, God of Israel, there is no God like you, in heaven or on earth, keeping covenant and showing steadfast love to your servants who walk before you with all their heart"* (ESV) No matter how mature, seasoned, or experienced others may have been, God's power was enabling me to choreograph, lead, teach, pray, and serve with compassion and love.

As the ministry was growing in number, I was growing in my understanding of ministry, in my ability to lead the ministry, in my faith, in my confidence, and in my knowledge of God's Word. Scripture memory kept me grounded in my walk with God. Every verse God gave me was planted in my heart, because I took God at His Word. Numbers 23:19 says, *"God is not a man, so he does not lie. He is not human, so he does not change his mind. Has he ever spoken and failed to act? Has he ever promised and not carried it through?"* (NLT). It is in trusting God that I was able to dance as a soloist before an entire congregation. It is in trusting God that I was able to lead different age groups in the dance including children, teenagers, and adults. It was in trusting God that I found favor with my pastor, who provided me with a budget for the dance ministry.

As God opened more doors in the ministry of movement, I trusted Him in more areas of my life, including with my singing. Because I loved to sing, I decided to take voice lessons at Dorolyn Academy of Music which was founded and directed by Dr. Dorothy Bounds. Through my voice teacher, I was introduced to Pastor Rosalyn Acevedo. Not only was she the founder and director of Divine Expressions Dance Ministry (DEM), but at that time, she also headed the first dance program at Dorolyn. As I got to know Pastor Rosalyn, I acquired a deeper biblical understanding and appreciation for the dance ministry. As we ministered together at different churches and events, I learned how to flow spontaneously in the dance through the movement of God's Spirit.

As my relationship with Pastor Rosalyn developed, she invited me to join the first dance class that she taught at Dorolyn Academy. I was asked to minister a solo at the first dance graduation, which I did. After I graduated from the first dance class, Pastor Rosalyn asked me to become one of the DEM dance teachers at Dorolyn Academy. This was a big step, but I rose to the occasion. I started out teaching the biblical foundation of dance class. Eventually, I taught other classes, including tambourine dancing, beginners' ballet, beginners' jazz, congregational and solo dancing, pageantry, and prophetic dancing. Pageantry dancing is done by a group of dancers in an orderly fashion, often in a procession, using flags, tambourines, banners, scarves, billows or other ministry tools to elaborately display who God is. Prophetic dancing refers to Holy Spirit-led spontaneous dancing accompanied by prophetic music, singing, or speaking intended to edify, exhort, or comfort the body of Christ. Overall, these classes were not just about teaching dance but about giving perspective on why we dance and why God is the Lord over the dance. Teaching these classes also encompassed ministering to students as they participated in Dorolyn's dance program.

After a couple of years, I encouraged members of the Rock Church Dance ministry to take classes at Dorolyn Academy. As Rock Church's ministers of movement grew in their understanding of dance ministry, I passed my leadership of the children's dance ministry to one of the other dance ministers. For about 12 years, I taught dance classes at Dorolyn while leading the teenage and adult dance ministries at Rock Church.

The dance ministry teams at Rock Church were being used by God to encourage the church through movement with expressions of God's love, power, hope, and salvation. The classes at Dorolyn Academy were being taught to activate the gifts and help develop students who felt called to the ministry of dance. As God was bringing the increase in these ministries in number, abilities, and spiritual understanding, my role was to continue to do my part as God did the rest. I had to continue to walk with Him and trust the work that He was doing in the people and the work He was doing in and through me. I had to walk in humility, in faith, in love, in God's strength, with confidence, and without being afraid of the new.

In the Bible, God had to encourage many of the people He called to serve to be strong and courageous, including Joshua, who struggled with courage. When Caleb and Joshua spied out the land of Canaan, which was to be conquered, they returned to the Israelites with a report that the land had powerful people and large fortified cities. Despite the report, Caleb and Joshua trusted God, but the other 10 spies doubted God and were afraid, which impacted Israel. Through God's strength, Joshua was able to lead the children of Israel into the Promised Land, defeat the enemies, conquer battles, and stay true to God.

Just like Joshua, I often faced challenges while leading the Rock Church dance ministry, which demanded strength and courage. I came up against rebellious people, fear of the unknown, and Satan attacking me mentally, physically, and through other circumstances. In all of this, I had to trust God through the process and hold on to His Word. If not, I could have died spiritually, or God's work in and through me could have been hindered. By God's strength and power, I overcame every obstacle that presented itself. Over the course of time, the Rock Church dance ministry rose to new levels of knowledge and experience.

After 13 years, God showed me that my time with Divine Expressions was coming to an end. It was time to enter a new season of ministry, but I did not know what that meant for me. At the same time, Divine Expressions' time with Dorolyn had also ended. This was a time of shifting not only for me but also for Dorolyn Academy of Music and DEM. Although I followed God's leading, this transition was still difficult for me because I had invested so much time in developing my relationship with the members of DEM. We ministered together. We dined together. We traveled together. We had fun together. We gleaned from each other, and we held each other accountable. Yet I had to be obedient to how God was leading me, no matter how difficult it was to leave the ministry.

Even with the transition, Dr. Bounds decided she wanted to continue the dance program at Dorolyn. She asked me to consider overseeing the program. I was unsure if this was truly God elevating me or even if it was God placing a new calling on my life. I was also unsure if I was ready to lead an emerging dance program at Dorolyn Academy of Music. Nonetheless, I said yes because I wanted to help a friend in need. Even though being asked to serve in that capacity was an honor and a privilege, leading the dance program at Dorolyn was never my interest or intent. In fact, after leading the program for a year, God made it clear to me that I was not moving in the direction He wanted me to go. So, out of obedience to how the Holy Spirit was leading me, I stepped down.

When I left Dorolyn, I felt a void. I had already separated from ministering with DEM, and now I was leaving the dance program at Dorolyn. Even though I had my Rock Church family, I still felt stagnated and alone as a dance ministry leader. After acquiring a deeper biblical understanding of the ministry of dance through DEM and through teaching the biblical foundational dance classes at Dorolyn, I yearned to go deeper into the ministry of dance but now I did not know where to find what I wanted and needed. I felt depleted and lonely and did not feel like I had much to offer the Rock Church dance ministry. It seems that when God is about to move in my life, He always places me in a position of being alone and having no one else to trust but Him.

I was not sure what God was saying to me at that time, because my hearing was muffled by my self-focus. One thing I knew for sure was that I was in a waiting period. In that waiting period, I decided to branch out and attend dance conferences. During the summer of 2008, I attended a dance conference in Chicago and one in New York. At the conference in New York, I saw and experienced a whole new perspective on the ministry of movement. The ministers of movement were dressed in what they called priestly garments. The teachings on the dance ministry were very theologically based. During my time in New York, I realized that God had not abandoned me but was orchestrating something new in my life through dance. If I had not stayed obedient to God's leading, I would not have been able to go through the doors that God was now opening for me.

In God's faithfulness, He heard my prayers and fulfilled my desires.

One of the guest speakers I met in New York was Dr. Pamela Scott. She connected me to her ministry, the Eagles International Training Institute (EITI), and through that ministry, I was challenged, stretched, and encouraged to personally dig deeper into the Word of God. From 2009 to now, I have taken EITI courses that have developed me as a godly woman, as a minister and as a leader. Through the EITI experience, God took me through the fire. It wasn't just about acquiring knowledge, but God worked on my heart and mind to bring deliverance and purification as needed so that my life in Him would be lived with greater spiritual understanding and my service to Him and His people would be done in love, compassion, humility and in excellence. God also broaden my perspective on outreach to consider the needs of the world and not just my church, community or city.

In my over 30 years of ministering in movement, God has taken me from starting a dance ministry in my church to joining the Divine Expression Dance Ministry, teaching biblical dance classes at Dorolyn Academy of Music, becoming part of an international ministry, EITI to embarking on new assignments and callings in the ministry of movement. I have been able to continue to grow, develop, and serve in His kingdom locally, nationally, and internationally, serving in places like the British Virgin Islands and Trinidad because of God's goodness, faithfulness, and desire to use me to bless others through the ministry of movement. Serving and growing spiritually through the ministry of movement and meeting and gleaning from phenomenal women and men of God has been a blessing. It is amazing how God brings the right people into our lives to help us fulfill the purpose He has for us. If we allow God to have the steering *will* of our lives, He will do the planting, watering, and growing. I know without a doubt that God's hand is on my life, and He continuously uses the gifts He has given me for His glory.

God called me to the ministry of movement. What has God called you to? No matter what area of ministry God has called you to (or is calling you to right now), remember that it is God who will do the work through you. God will lead, protect, provide, direct, open and close doors, and bring the increase. Our responsibility is to say yes, even when we feel uncomfortable or uncertain about what God is doing. We must be willing to trust and wait on Him.

TAKING A DEEPER DIVE

1) What do you remember about accepting Jesus as your Lord and Savior?

   _____
   _____
   _____
   _____

2) In what way is God asking you to wait on Him?

   _____
   _____
   _____
   _____

3) In what way is God asking you to trust Him?

   _____
   _____
   _____
   _____

4) Is it difficult to say yes to God? Why or why not?

   _____
   _____
   _____
   _____

CHAPTER 2

CREATED FOR GOD'S PURPOSE

"For we are God's handiwork, created in Christ Jesus to do good works, which God prepared in advance for us to do."
(Ephesians 2:10 NIV)

In Rick Warren's book *The Purpose Driven Life*, he says, "The purpose of your life is far greater than your own personal fulfillment, your peace of mind, or even your happiness. It's far greater than your family, your career, or even your wildest dreams and ambitions. If you want to know why you were placed on this planet, you must begin with God. You were born *by* his purpose and *for* his purpose."[3]

Let's consider these three facets to take a closer look at God's purpose for creating you and me: God created you and me because it was part of His plan, God created you and me out of love, and God created you and me to glorify Him.

CREATED AS PART OF GOD'S PLAN

"'For I know the plans I have for you,' declares the LORD, 'plans to prosper you and not to harm you, plans to give you hope and a future.'"
Jeremiah 29:11 (NIV)

Before the world was created, God existed. God is the Alpha and Omega and is not defined by time, space, or matter. He knows the beginning and end of all things. God already had a plan for the layout of the design of the world. God already had a plan for you and me even before the foundation of the world. "God is not just creating, but He is assigning purpose," stated Rock Church's Sunday school teacher, Steve McIlrath. Consider the prophet Jeremiah. Jeremiah was called to ministry before he was born. He was told by God, *"Before I formed you in the womb, I knew you before you were born, I set you apart; I appointed you as a prophet to the nations"* (Jeremiah 1:5 NIV). God already planned for Jeremiah to be a prophet even before he was born. God knew the purpose that He wanted Jeremiah to fulfill, and God knows the purpose that He wants you and me to fulfill. We are connected to the Creator in our purpose.

Through Jesus Christ, man was created. Colossians 1:16 says, *"For in him all things were created: things in heaven and on earth, visible and invisible, whether thrones, powers, rulers, or authorities; all things have been created through him and for him"* (NIV). Through Christ, we were chosen to be holy and blameless before the world's creation and to be adopted as God's sons and daughters. God created us knowing that we would sin and would need a Savior to redeem us from our sins. God already had in mind that Jesus would be the sacrificial lamb to redeem the world from sin by sacrificing His precious blood on the cross. We are justified through Christ Jesus. Without Jesus, the creation of man, God's relationship with man, the forgiveness of man, and eternal life would not be possible.

CREATED OUT OF GOD'S LOVE

*"God surveyed all he had made and said,
'I love it!' For it pleased him greatly…"*
(Genesis 1:31 TPT)

We are God's dearly loved children, and He loves us as a perfect Father. God's love existed before time because God is love. Before the beginning of creation, there was love between God and Jesus. God created you and me with love and desires a relationship with us. Just as the Bible refers to love in 1 Corinthians 13 as being patient, kind, not envious, not boastful, not proud, not dishonoring, not self-seeking, not easily angered, keeping no record of wrongs, not delighting in evil, never failing but rejoicing with the truth, always protecting, always trusting, always hoping, and always persevering, so is God, our Creator.

Just as God loves us, He wants us to love Him and love others. Love is so important to God that He has given us two great commandments. The first is "Love the Lord your God with all your heart and with all your soul and with all your mind." The second is "Love your neighbor as yourself." We are to love others just as much as we love ourselves. We show love to others through our willingness to forgive and serve others.

One of the ways that God has demonstrated His love to us is by creating us in His image. We resemble God mentally, morally, and socially. He created us to be like Him in our personalities, emotions, and intellect. God did not create us as robots but to be functional. We have His intellect to think, reason, make decisions, invent, and create. We have the mind of Christ to know the difference between good and evil and the inner workings of the Holy Spirit to help us reflect God's holiness. God gives us the strength to be patient, kind, humble, respectful, compassionate, honest, forgiving, and empathetic. These deeds could be performed conditionally or pridefully in our strength, but God gets the glory when they are done through His strength.

CREATED TO GLORIFY GOD

Glorify God Through Praise

The next time you can enjoy the outdoors, look around. Take note of the radiant sun, the blue skies, the swaying of the tree branches, and the blooming flowers. Listen to the chirping birds and feel the caress of the gentle, fresh wind as it touches your face. What you are experiencing is God through nature. You are experiencing the sights and sounds of God through His creations. God's magnificence and splendor are being displayed as nature functions in the way that God purposed it to function.

God created all things to glorify Him or, in other words, to honor Him with praise, admiration, or worship. When we see God's glory in nature, we see how amazing and wonderful God is. We are seeing His power and majestic beauty.

If God is glorified in nature, how much more is He glorified through humankind? Our responsibility as God's children is to glorify God through praise and worship. Psalm 150:6 says, *"Let everything that has breath praise the Lord. Praise the Lord"* (NIV). Jesus told the Pharisees that if the people had kept quiet, he would have gotten the stones to praise him (Luke 19:36-40). Whether we praise God in words, in song, in dance, by playing an instrument, by painting, through poetry or writing, by lifting our hands, or by other means, God's presence will be manifested. As the Word says, this is when the glory of God will fall. This is when miracles, signs, and wonders can manifest, like someone receiving Christ or someone being healed or delivered. God inhabits the praises of His people (Psalm 22:3). God desires our praise and seeks those who will worship Him in spirit and truth, as stated in John 4:23-24.

Glorify God by Obeying His Word

We also glorify God when we obey His Word. Obedience to God's Word is how we grow personally and draw closer to God. In 1 John 2:5, it says, *"But whoever keeps His word, truly the love of God is perfected in him. By this we know that we are in Him"* (NKJV). "God wants us to hear His Word, to know His Word, to trust His Word, and to keep His Word…. We can only keep His Word if we trust His Word. We can only trust His Word if we hear His Word, for *'faith comes by hearing, and hearing by the Word of God.'* And we can only keep His Word if we hear, know, and believe in our hearts ALL that God has said in and through His Holy Word."[4]

Glorify God by Proclaiming His Truth

God has given us the eyes to see His magnificence and the words to proclaim His Truth. Concerning the Bible, "proclaim" signifies "making a public announcement or sharing the good news."[5] We are all called to proclaim God's Truth about sin, love, judgment, repentance, and salvation to others. When discussing our faith with others, we proclaim God's Truth. It is not only in the spoken word that we do so but also in the songs that we sing or dance to proclaim the attributes and power of God. We use our gifts to proclaim God's Truth through us. Luke 4:18 says, *"The Spirit of the Lord is on me, because he has anointed me to proclaim good news to the poor. He has sent me to proclaim freedom for the prisoners and recovery of sight for the blind, to set the oppressed free"* (NIV). We are to be an example of Christ through our lives and through our service. Because God's Holy Spirit dwells inside of us, we carry His glory with us. No matter where we go or where God positions us, we can proclaim His truth through our walk, talk, and actions.

Glorify God by Using Your Authority

When God blessed Adam and Eve and said to them in Genesis 1:28, *"Be fruitful, and multiply, and replenish the earth, and subdue it"* (KJV), He was giving them a command and a responsibility to rule over the earth. He was telling them to oversee and manage the earth's resources. God gave them the authority to take control of, exercise power over, and dominate the earth. God has called us to lead or take charge. Man is to serve as the king of the earth. What do kings do? They lead. They rule. They govern. They make life-changing decisions. They are problem solvers, providers, overseers, and inventors. They hold responsibility for the lives of others. I once heard a politician say, "Rule with a servant's heart and lead with the heart of a king." We must never forget that we lead as servants.

The body of Christ is who will conduct God's work in the world. What we accomplish on earth is what we put into action and what God allows us to accomplish. God has given us gifts so that we can serve in God's kingdom and demonstrate the love of Christ. Every purpose that we fulfill is a privilege and should not be a chore. Serving should not be done out of guilt or obligation but cheerfully. Serving is about utilizing our gifts, talents, and abilities to glorify God. Using our gifts is God's love in action. We are giving from what God has given us. Nothing is ours; everything about us belongs to God.

Fan Into Flame

TAKING A DEEPER DIVE

1) How has God shown His love to you?

   _____
   _____
   _____
   _____

2) In what ways do you show love to others?

   _____
   _____
   _____
   _____

3) How have others benefited from the love you have shown?

   _____
   _____
   _____
   _____

4) In what ways do you think you bring glory to God?

   _____
   _____
   _____
   _____

CHAPTER 3

GIFTED FOR GOD'S PURPOSE

"Your Kingdom purpose is the service God has gifted you to perform, that has eternal value. More specifically, your Kingdom purpose is that thing you do, that you don't do—but that God does through you."[6]

Whenever I receive a gift wrapped in festive paper and sealed with a beautiful ribbon or bow, I think about the time, the love, and the thoughtfulness of the person who prepared that gift for me. Even before I open the gift, my heart is emotionally grateful for the generosity shown. God has created each of us as a special gift to the earth. We are beautifully designed and wrapped in the skin that God chose for us. We are all wrapped differently, which makes each of us so unique as a person and in God's eyes. The ribbon or bow is that stamp of completion, sealing the gift with a finishing touch of beauty.

God has sealed us with the beauty of His Holy Spirit, which is the finishing touch of being packaged as a new person in Christ Jesus.

Sometimes, when I open a gift, I keep the wrapping paper or ribbon because the paper's design and the ribbon's color are so attractive to me. As God's gift, we must know and hold on to who we are and how God has designed us. We have mirrors and people in our lives to remind us of the beautiful wrapping God has placed us in. When we look in the mirror, we look at God's beautiful creation whom God has loved, gifted, and given purpose. How do you see yourself? Are you comfortable with who you are? Have you considered how God sees you?

WHO ARE YOU?

Our identity answers the question "Who are you?" It stems from what is inside of us. According to *Psychology Today*, "identity encompasses the values people hold, which dictate the choices they make. An identity contains multiple roles—such as a mother, teacher, and U.S. citizen—and each role holds meaning and expectations that are internalized into one's identity. Identity continues to evolve over the course of an individual's life." *Psychology Today* discusses that your identity is formed by "discovering and developing one's potential, choosing one's purpose in life, and finding opportunities to exercise that potential and purpose. Identity is also influenced by parents and peers during childhood and experimentation in adolescence."[7]

When we receive Jesus Christ into our lives, our identity is redefined by who we are in Him. 2 Corinthians 5:17 says, *"This means that anyone who belongs to Christ has become a new person. The old life is gone; a new life has begun!"* (NLT). We now live a life of faith in God, guided by the Holy Spirit instead of the flesh. As we get to know Christ, we get to know who we are. We must pattern our lives after Christ, who demonstrated to us how to live a godly life on earth. When we surrender our lives to Christ, we start talking, acting, and thinking like Christ, exemplifying the true person God desires us to be. God is purifying the hearts and minds of the old self that was contaminated by the stains of the world and all the lies that the enemy planted within us. God is giving us beauty instead of ashes, joy instead of mourning, strength instead of fear, wholeness instead of brokenness, praise instead of hopelessness, and peace instead of anxiety.

As we accept God's truths by faith, we regain the power and identity God had already established for us. Psalm 139 speaks about God creating our inmost being and says that we were fearfully and wonderfully made. 1 Peter 2:9 says that we are *"a chosen people, a royal priesthood, a holy nation, God's special possession"* (NIV). 1 Corinthians 6:19 reminds us that our bodies are the temples within which God's Holy Spirit dwells. 2 Corinthians 5:20 says we are ambassadors of Christ. John 1:12 states that we are children of God, and Romans 8:17 says that we are heirs of God and co-heirs with Christ. Ephesians 1:4 calls us holy and blameless. Psalm 17:8 says that we are the apple of God's eye. God is doing the work to shape us into the person He designed us to be. We cannot allow others to define who we are; we must believe and accept our profile that has been laid out in God's Word. Believing and accepting who we are and how God has created us will allow us to soar in our purpose, having confidence that comes from God to accomplish everything He has planned for us to do.

GOD KNOWS BEST

As far back as the 1300s, gifts were wrapped in fabric to symbolize protection and good luck. When the wise men from the East brought gifts of gold, frankincense, and myrrh to honor the birth of baby Jesus, they did not just set the gifts on the ground, but they offered them in treasure chests as a protective covering. Traditionally, we often place our gifts in boxes to protect them from getting damaged. God is the covering and protection of us, His special gift. God not only protects us, His gift, but also protects the gifts that He has given us. In addition, He protects our physical, emotional, mental, and spiritual well-being through the comfort of His Word and His power at work in our lives. So, who is this God who has gifted us and cares for us?

Who Is God?

When we come to know God for ourselves, we will see Him as our protector and as our Father, our physician, our friend, our peace, our comforter, and everything we need to sustain us for eternity. In scripture, God is characterized as good, gracious, merciful, faithful, holy, omniscient, omnipresent, omnipotent, just, perfect, and unchanging. God is also referred to as the "Sovereign Lord," the "Living God," the "Everlasting God"; Adonai, which means "Lord Master"; Elohim, which means "the Creator"; El Shaddai, which means "God Almighty"; and Jehovah-Jireh, which means "the Lord, our Provider." Without knowing God for ourselves, we would not be able to appreciate who He is and what He does. When we personally know God's character and His nature, then we can embrace Him as the lover of our soul, the Father to the fatherless, and the friend to the friendless. When we come to know God, we become more connected in seeing the way He sees, hearing the way He hears, and speaking the way He would want us to speak. We become familiar with the heart of God.

How Does God See Us?

We should know not only who God is but also how God sees us. God knows us better than we know ourselves. God knows our thoughts and our ways. There is nothing about us that is hidden from Him. Luke 12:6 says that there is no sparrow that God has forgotten. If God has not forgotten about the sparrow, He has not forgotten about you. Although we may be unable to tell one sparrow from the next, God knows each one intimately and provides for them all. How much more consideration does God give to each of us? God knows how valuable we are. We are so valuable to God that He even knows the number of hair strands on our heads. *"See what great love the Father has lavished on us, that we should be called children of God! And that is what we are!"* (1 John 3:1 NIV). God has crowned us with glory and honor. We are His special possession.

God sees us differently from how we see ourselves. To God, we are precious and irreplaceable. In John 15:15, Jesus says, *"No longer do I call you servants, for the servant does not know what his master is doing; but I have called you friends, for all that I have heard from my Father I have made known to you"* (ESV) God sees us through the lens of His Son, Jesus, who became our sin and burnt offerings. As our sin offering, Jesus took on our sins so that His righteousness was transferred to us. As our burnt offering, Jesus' righteousness, excellence, beauty, and perfection have been transferred to us. All that Jesus is before God, we become when we receive Him as our Lord and Savior.[8]

Undoubtedly, we are important to God. When we discredit ourselves, we are discrediting the one who created us. We are speaking against everything God proclaims us to be. When we doubt our abilities, we say we lack faith in what God can do through us. When we fail to use our gifts, we say what God has given us is not important. While we look at ourselves and see all our human limitations, God looks at us and sees all the potential and greatness that He has put in us. He is waiting on us, His Beloved, to "be" who He has blessed us to "be" through His love.

BEYOND THE GIFT

My Testimony

Do you remember the encounter that Jesus, a Jew, had with the Samaritan woman? Traveling from Jerusalem to Galilee, Jesus and His disciples took a shorter route through Samaria, which was Jesus' plan so that he could meet the woman at the well. While the disciples went to purchase food at the village of Sychar, Jesus conversed with a Samaritan woman who had come to Jacob's Well to draw water. Jesus asked her for a drink. The woman questioned why Jesus would ask her, a social outcast, for a drink. Jesus was breaking three Jewish laws by speaking to the woman, associating with a Samaritan, and asking her for a drink of water. But Jesus was more concerned about the woman's soul than the Jewish laws, and he offered her the gift of salvation (John 4:1-26).

To reach people with the love of Christ, we need to go where the people are. Some people may never set foot inside the door of a church. Whether we are in the church or outside it, our mission is to serve all people. God wants to reach all people working through the gifts, talents, and abilities that He has given us to touch hearts.

While working in the corporate world, I received another call from God. That call was to have an influence on young people's lives through a teaching career. Here is my story of how I accepted the call to become a high school math teacher:

Math was always my favorite and easiest subject in elementary and high school. But even though I enjoyed math, I did not enjoy my math classes. My teachers made math seem difficult and boring. At the age of 14, I remember saying that I would never become a teacher because that type of career did not seem appealing. My interest in math and science resulted in me pursuing a bachelor's degree in mechanical engineering. According to statistics, this accomplishment was and still is uncommon for an African American female growing up in a single-parent home and in an under-resourced community. Nonetheless, God made it possible. Against all odds, God blessed me with a career in mechanical engineering, giving me exposure to the type of people, places, and things that I had never experienced before. I was incredibly grateful for every door God had opened for me. At the same time, I had to deal with every struggle that came with being an African American female in a male-dominated career.

Having experienced a new life in Christ that involved ministering in the dance, singing in the choir, and serving as a youth leader at my church, I had now embarked on a career painted by a historical struggle that has haunted Black people and women for many decades: the struggle for equality. What I did not realize at that time was that God was exposing me to the world with all its brokenness and working out the plans He had for my life at the same time. His plans were more meaningful than any struggle I would experience at my job. Although I felt like a "square peg in a round hole" in the corporate world, God used that experience to build my character and prepare me for what was to come. God was also using me to be a light in a work environment that consisted of men with narcissistic behavior. If I reached one person through sharing my faith, the experience was worth it.

A few of my coworkers saw that I was different. They saw me as humble and helpful rather than prideful and competitive. Some coworkers asked me if I had ever considered teaching or a trainer position. They saw an ability in me that I did not see in myself. I received comments about being a good trainer from my coworkers and friends. Church members were also complimenting me on being a good teacher. As I kept receiving encouraging words about my abilities in teaching and training, I began to question what God was trying to say to me through these people. I saw it as strange that people from different spheres of my life perceived me similarly.

Unexpectedly, I received an email from Chicago Public Schools (CPS) around the same time I was getting these comments from people. The email offered me an opportunity to change careers through a program called Teachers for Chicago. To this day, I do not know how CPS received my email address or even knew of me. The email stated that my tuition would be paid in full if I was willing to obtain a master's degree in education while simultaneously teaching at a CPS school. I decided to pursue the offer. I successfully passed the interviewing process, and I was also given the privilege to choose the high school where I wanted to teach. For two years, I took evening classes at St. Xavier University, and taught math during the day at John F. Kennedy High School. I did not have any prior teaching experience. I then successfully completed the process to become a certified teacher. Without a doubt, I knew that God had made all that I was experiencing possible.

Why would God call me to a new career in teaching when I never intended to become a math teacher, and I was just "getting my feet wet" as a mechanical engineer? Even though teaching was not my goal, dream, or desire, God had a bigger plan in mind that involved more than I could have imagined. It was just like how Jesus and the disciples could have continued their travel from Jerusalem to Galilee in the direction they were going, but Jesus changed course for the sake of the Samaritan. Jesus knew that He would be the only one to reach her and let her know that she was loved, accepted, and forgiven, and that she had the chance to receive eternal life with the Father. Even though I did not know what I would be walking into as a teacher, God knew of the students who were hurting, living in abusive homes, dealing with low self-esteem and mental illnesses, feeling hopeless and unloved, and struggling to understand math. God chose me to be one of the vessels that would impact young people's lives for the cause of Christ. In my first year of teaching, I will never forget how one of my ninth-grade students cried because she said she had never done well or understood math until she took my class. Because of her previous teachers, she had developed a fear that paralyzed her ability to learn math. Seeing God use me in this young lady's life and in so many other students' lives has been the inspiration that has kept me serving in the field of education for 28 years.

Even though some people thought that I was insane to make a drastic career change, I never looked back or had regrets about my decision because it was all for His glory and at the same time, a fulfilling experience. God enabled me to become a teacher and then allowed me to be elevated in this career with blessings on top of blessings. Through another CPS program, I was given another opportunity to receive a second Master of Arts degree in school leadership at Concordia University. This degree took one year and allowed me to be considered for an assistant principal or principal position. Not only was I blessed with some of the professors coming to my high school in the evening to teach their courses, so I didn't have to travel to Concordia, I was also able to take the classes with a cohort group of teachers at my high school, which made the endeavor more exciting and attainable.

I decided not to pursue the assistant principalship or the principalship. Instead, God allowed me to serve for one year as an Instructional Support Leader in math for 25 elementary schools. I mentored principals and assistant principals and coached math teachers. After that experience, I went on to become a STEM (Science, Technology, Engineering, and Math) Specialist for an elementary school for five years and a STEAM (Science, Technology, Engineering, Art, and Math) Specialist for a high school for four years, incorporating my background and experience in mechanical engineering to foster the ideas and activities that I implemented for the school.

I am thankful that God uses people, experiences, and places to speak into our lives. God has done tremendous work in my life, using the gifts He gave me to bless others. God has shown me that I have a purpose. He has reminded me that all the gifts He gives us are important. What God has done for me, He wants to do for you. You cannot take for granted your gifts, or the transitions that may be happening in your life. God may be repositioning you for a greater purpose. Be sensitive to how God speaks in your life, because you do not want to miss your blessings. Even though it may be difficult, we must trust God for what will come next. It was not until I said yes to accepting Christ into my life that I could understand His will for me. It was not until I said yes to the calling to dance for Him that the dance ministry began to take form and prosper. When I said yes to the call, I was saying to God that I was ready to be used by Him. It is your choice to say yes to God's will, but when you do, your life will never be the same.

TAKING A DEEPER DIVE

1) How do you see yourself?

   _____
   _____
   _____
   _____

2) Are you comfortable with who you are? Why or why not?

   _____
   _____
   _____
   _____

3) How do you think God sees you?

   _____
   _____
   _____
   _____

4) In what ways has God required you, or is now requiring you, to make a shift?

   _____
   _____
   _____
   _____

CHAPTER 4

OVERFLOWING WITH GOD'S GIFTS

BEING CALLED

In Matthew 22:14, Jesus says, *"For many are called, but few are chosen"* (ESV). This verse encapsulates the parable Jesus shared with the crowd about a king who invited many people to attend his son's wedding banquet, but no one showed up. People either ignored the invitation, refused it, or were preoccupied with their own affairs. The king concluded that those people he invited were not worthy to attend the wedding banquet, so invitations were given out again, this time to anyone the king's servants met on the streets.

The people on the streets responded positively to the invitation and were guests at the wedding. However, one guest did not dress in the appropriate wedding clothes and was thrown outside into the darkness. The "called" received the initial invitation, while the "chosen" accepted the invitation and responded appropriately.

The point is this: Being called, invited, or summoned by God is always for a purpose. Although everyone has ears to hear the call, only a few people listen and respond. Others refuse or ignore the call, are preoccupied with their own affairs, or do not respond appropriately. Those people will not be found worthy of the call.

God's first invitation or calling is not exclusive but goes out to all people, regardless of background or circumstances. God first "calls" or invites us to have a relationship with Him by becoming followers of Jesus. The ones who wholeheartedly accept the calling or invitation are saying yes to the calling and yes to living for Jesus. They are the ones whom God will be able to use to be effective in His kingdom.

God's call is not just to a relationship with Him but also to our relationships with others. God forms families, communities, and churches to support and encourage one another. As Ecclesiastes 4:9-10 states, *"Two are better than one because they have a good return for their labor; for if either of them falls, the one will lift up his companion. But woe to the one who falls when there is not another to lift him up!"* (NASB). Hebrews 10:24 says, "And let us consider how to stir up one another to love and good works, not neglecting to meet together, as is the habit of some, but encouraging one another, and all the more as you see the Day drawing near" (ESV). This scripture emphasizes that God is a God of relationships and community and that it is important not to be alone. Proverbs 27:17 says, *"As iron sharpens iron, so one person sharpens another"* (NIV). We are not called to serve God's people in isolation; we need accountability. In times of loneliness or feeling isolated, Satan will try to steer us away from God's calling but being part of a community can help us stay strong, become more confident and progress in whatever God has called us to do.

We are also called to serve in God's kingdom in various roles, whether at home, in church, in school, in vocations, or in professions. In the video series from the "God. Gifts. You." website by Shirley Giles Davis, she says, "Calling is really about God saying, 'I have a plan, and it involves you, and it involves us.' God guides us, walks with us, and enables us to do what He calls us to do." God has given us gifts to fulfill an assignment that He has called us to do on this earth. People can see God's love in action when we use the gifts God has given us to fulfill our calling.

GOD'S NATURAL GIFTS

When I think of a gift, I think of something willingly given without expecting anything in return. No matter what is in the box, it is valuable to me because someone took the time to make or purchase it for me. God took the time to choose the gift He would put inside each of us. Our gifts are not a coincidence but thoughtfully chosen by our Father according to His plan for our lives.

God has freely given all humankind many gifts to enable us to function in our humanness, partake in pleasure, and serve others. In fact, James 1:17 reminds us that *"whatever is good and perfect is a gift coming down to us from God our Father"* (NLT). As we open our gifts, let us remember that God is the one who gave them to us. Let us thank God for our gifts and ask Him how He wants us to use them. Every gift that God has given has equal value to Him and should be equally valued by us. In addition to giving us such gifts as His unconditional love, salvation, eternal life, and grace and mercy, God has also given us natural gifts and talents.

Before birth, we were predestined to receive gifts. Natural gifts include the ability to see, hear, speak, walk, and talk. They also include having the aptitude to do something or the ability to learn something. For example, a person may have the aptitude to teach, play a sport, learn a language, or work with their hands. A talent is a natural skill or ability to do something without needing training. Some people have talents in singing, dancing, public speaking, and writing poetry. God can use our natural talents, skills, and abilities to serve Him if we are willing.

Our natural gifts go beyond meeting our personal needs to include ministering to the needs of others. When we serve people, we indirectly serve God, because all we do brings glory to His name. We are not only bringing joy and pleasure to those who are being illuminated by our giftings, but we also bring joy and pleasure to God. God expects us to assume ownership and use the skills and talents He has given us. Even if our talents and abilities seem small to us, they can be a blessing to others.

GOD'S FRUIT OF THE SPIRIT

Jesus said in John 14:26, "But the Helper, the Holy Spirit, whom the Father will send in My name, He will teach you all things, and bring to your remembrance all things that I said to you" (NKJV). It is a blessing to know that when we receive Christ in our lives, we receive the gift of the Holy Spirit. God has given us the gift of the Holy Spirit as our Helper, helping us to become more like Jesus Christ and helping us in every other aspect of our lives. When we are sealed with the Holy Spirit, we always have the presence of God with us because He dwells inside of us. The Word of God tells us that the Holy Spirit is our comforter, counselor, and peace. The Holy Spirit empowers us. We are given strength or power in our innermost being through the Holy Spirit working in us. Valerie Murray writes, "The Holy Spirit empowers us, purifies us, reveals truth, and unites us so we can bring glory to God."[9]

From Got Questions, we learn that "in the Bible, the word *fruit* is often used to describe a person's outward actions that result from the condition of the heart. Good fruit is that which is produced by the Holy Spirit."[10] Galatians 5:22-23 tells us that the good fruit produced by the Holy Spirit is *"love, joy, peace, forbearance, kindness, goodness, faithfulness, gentleness and self-control"* (NIV). In whatever capacity we serve in God's kingdom, we want people to see the fruit of the Spirit flowing and evident in our lives. It is the fruit of the Spirit that produces the godliness in us. We want the fruit flowing in our lives because we want to reflect Jesus. We want people to see Jesus' power working in our weakness. We want people to see the love of Christ shown with kind, compassionate, and giving hearts. We want people to see His grace covering our sins. We want people to see our oneness with God. Apart from the Holy Spirit, we cannot bear the fruit of the Spirit.

GOD'S SPIRITUAL GIFTS

Using our natural gifts can be a vehicle to open the door for spiritual gifts. Every believer or follower of Christ has received a spiritual gift from God to serve the body of Christ. "Spiritual gifts are special abilities, talents, or capacities given to individual Christians by the Holy Spirit for the purpose of serving God and others within the Christian community. These gifts are not natural talents or skills, but supernatural endowments provided by God's grace. They are meant to be used to build up the body of Christ, which is the community of believers."[11]

Every spiritual gift serves a purpose and displays who God is. For example, the spiritual gift of healing tells us that God is a healer and is working through the person with the gift of healing as His vessel to heal someone. God has called us and equipped us with spiritual gifts so that we can take an active role in the church. We each exercise the power of our spiritual gift based on our faith in our Heavenly Father. Spiritual gifts cannot be perfected but can be increased as they are used.

In the New Testament, the phrase "spiritual gift" is rooted in two words meaning "God's grace and His Holy Spirit." Paul and Peter referred to spiritual gifts as "charismata," which means the grace of God, or "pneumatikos" in Greek, meaning of or relating to the Spirit.[12] With a spiritual gift, we serve God by serving the church. We serve out of love and not out of guilt or obligation. When people in your local church know your spiritual gifts, they can attest to how they are edified by it. Spiritual gifts are effective if they are used for God's glory and not our own.

"There are different kinds of gifts, but the same Spirit distributes them. There are different kinds of service, but the same Lord. There are different kinds of working, but in all of them and in everyone it is the same God at work. Now to each one the manifestation of the Spirit is given for the common good" (1 Corinthians 12:4-7 NIV). Through the work of the Holy Spirit, we use our spiritual gifts to manifest God's active presence in the world, especially in the church.[13]

Christianity.com categorizes spiritual gifts into three categories based on Scripture. These gifts are listed as ministry gifts, manifestation gifts and motivational gifts. Ministry gifts are the way God works with believers to minister or ad-minister the love, grace and truth of God to others.[14] These ministering gifts are listed in Ephesians 4:11-13 and 1 Corinthians 12:28. Ephesians 4:11-13 says, *"And He Himself gave some to be apostles, some prophets, some evangelists, and some pastors and teachers, for the equipping of the saints for the work of ministry, for the edifying of the body of Christ, till we all come to the unity of the faith and of the knowledge of the Son of God, to a perfect man, to the measure of the stature of the fullness of Christ*" (NKJV). Everyone may not possess one of these five-fold ministry gifts but have other gifts of helping as found in 1 Corinthians 12:28: "And God has appointed these in the church: first apostles, second prophets, third teachers, after that miracles, then gifts of healings, helps, administrations, varieties of tongues" (NKJV). From these passages, we can derive the ministry gifts which are Apostles, Prophets, Evangelists, Pastors, Teachers and Helpers.

The second category of spiritual gifts are manifestation gifts which are "supernatural demonstrations of the Holy Spirit's presence and power".[15] Due to the controversy and misunderstandings surrounding the use of these gifts, some of these gifts are either ignored, rejected or overemphasized in some denominations of Christianity. The manifestation spiritual gifts of the Holy Spirit are found in 1 Corinthians 12: 7-11 which says, *"But the manifestation of the Spirit is given to each one for the profit of all: for to one is given the word of wisdom through the Spirit, to another the word of knowledge through the same Spirit, to another faith by the same Spirit, to another gifts of healings by the same Spirit, to another the working of miracles, to another prophecy, to another discerning of spirits, to another different kinds of tongues, to another the interpretation of tongues. But one and the same Spirit works all these things, distributing to each one individually as He wills"* (NKJV).

The nine manifestation spiritual gifts are words of wisdom, words of knowledge, faith, gifts of healing, working of miracles, prophecy, discerning of spirits, speaking in tongue and interpretation of tongue.

The final category of spiritual gifts is motivational spiritual gifts. "The motivational gifts are how the Spirit of grace moves through us, motivating our words and actions. It's a filter we're given for our perspective, shaping how we relate to and serve others."[16] Romans 12:6-8 says, *"We have different gifts, according to the grace given to each of us. If your gift is prophesying, then prophesy in accordance with your faith; if it is serving, then serve; if it is teaching, then teach; if it is to encourage, then give encouragement; if it is giving, then give generously; if it is to lead, do it diligently; if it is to show mercy, do it cheerfully"* (NIV). The motivational spiritual gifts from this passage are prophesying, serving, teaching, encouraging, giving, leading and mercy.

In summary, the spiritual gifts that I found in scripture are the following:

> Apostle, Prophet, Evangelist, Pastor, Teacher, Helps, Miracles, Wisdom, Knowledge, Faith, Gifts of Healing, Workers of Miracles, Prophecy, Discernment of Spirits, Speaking in Tongues, Interpretation of Tongues, Serving, Teaching, Encouragement, Giving, Leadership, Mercy, and Administration.

A description of each spiritual gift can be found in the appendix section of this book.

It is only through God that we can obtain a better understanding of the spiritual gifts. God has given us the Holy Spirit to teach us on what is truth. God has given us His Word as the highest authority on all matter. "Knowing and understanding the gifts that the Holy Spirit has given you to use gives you purpose in God's Kingdom. Spiritual gifts left unused do a disservice to the Church and hinder the believer from flourishing in their faith. This is such an identity issue, really. When we know who we are (and how we've been uniquely gifted) then we know what to do (how to glorify God by serving His Church)."[17]

The Unexpected Gifts

My Testimony

Just like you, I wanted to know what my spiritual gifts were. I have taken spiritual gift assessments and found that our gifts and callings can change as God brings us through different seasons in our lives. When I was leading the dance ministry, God deposited in me every natural and spiritual gift I needed to lead the ministry effectively: dancing, prophetic dancing, teaching, administration, serving, helping, giving, encouragement, mercy, leadership, and creativity. Unexpectedly, I was also blessed with the spiritual gifts of prophecy and speaking in tongues. The gift of prophecy refers to the ability to speak forth a message from God's Word that edifies, exhorts, and/or comforts the body.[18] When I started flowing in the prophetic dance, I would sense

God directing me in movement. This experience made me more sensitive to the Holy Spirit's leading and more sensitive to hearing God speak in the Spirit.

When Rock Church was under the pastoral leadership of Pastor Lincoln Washington, there was a breakthrough ministry (as referred to by Pastor Lincoln). Through that ministry, I was taught how to minister to people seeking prayer when they came to the altar. Part of the teaching came from watching and helping Pastor Lincoln at the altar. The other part of the teaching came through the Holy Spirit's empowerment and guidance. When Pastor Lincoln gave an altar call toward the end of the service, I would join the other leaders at the altar, and we would lay hands on those at the altar and pray for them. During those times and as the Holy Spirit moved, God started giving me a prophetic word to speak over some of the people I would pray for.

Some gifts we receive come to us because of our faith in God. I once heard a TV evangelist say, "To stir up our gifts is to stir up faith. Everything God plans to do for us is already planned but must be activated by faith. Growing in our faith will enable us to operate from the spiritual and not just from the natural. God will not attach us to the spiritual apart from faith." James 2:17-18 says, *"Thus also faith by itself, if it does not have works, is dead. But someone will say, 'You have faith, and I have works.' Show me your faith without your works, and I will show you my faith by my works"* (NKJV).

Another gift that was given to me was speaking in tongues, also known in some Christian circles as "speaking in a heavenly language." Speaking in tongues refers to "the ability to speak in unknown languages as a form of prayer or communication with God."[19] I remember taking a class at another church that taught intercessory prayer. During the last session of that class, they wanted us to speak in tongues. At that time, I did not know how to speak in tongues, nor was I interested in doing so. I left the class because I did not want to be pressured into speaking in tongues. In my bewilderment, I decided to study scriptures that spoke about speaking in tongues. I also prayed and said to God that if He wants me to speak in tongues, He will have to do it, because I will not try to make myself do it.

A month later, my church had a women's retreat. After the evening service at the retreat ended, several women, including myself, remained with the guest speaker to lay hands and pray over a lady experiencing spiritual warfare. We laid hands on her and prayed over her for about an hour. While praying for the lady, I started to speak in tongues. It was beyond my control, and I could not stop the process. God was in control. That was a God moment that I will never forget. Amazingly, God answered my prayers, and I spoke in tongues. God did it! God demonstrated His faithfulness, provisions, and power working in me to enable me to speak in an unknown language. Since then, I have continued to speak in tongues, which I now see as a blessing and a privilege.

A pastor who speaks in tongues said that when you speak in tongues, you can pray and fight in prayer for multiple things in one sentence, versus praying with understanding for each concern one by one. From my experience of speaking in tongues, praying in the Spirit is beyond the depth of my understanding. Romans 8:26 says, *"We do not know what we ought to pray for, but the Spirit himself intercedes for us through wordless groans"* (NIV). When I speak in tongue, I do not know what I am saying because I do not have the gift of interpreting tongues, but the Holy Spirit gives me what to say, and in the process, God is renewing my mind and refreshing my spirit. As I stay yielded to the Spirit, God directs me in my thoughts, and what I pray in my natural language comes more freely and intentionally after speaking in tongues. Speaking in tongues provides me with a constant reminder that God is present with me and constantly at work in my life.

There is a time for speaking in tongues in public and in private. When it is done in private, it is for the edification of our own soul. When it is done in public, it is because there is someone there with the gift of interpretation of tongues, or it is a testimony to others of the manifestations of God's power at work during times of prayer, prophecy, or ministry.

God has distributed spiritual gifts to all believers. It is God's plan for us to function together, grow in faith, grow in love, grow in character, be unified in purpose with one heart and one mind centered on Jesus, and use our spiritual gifts for His glory. Every gift is needed to help unify and build the church. When the church works together and uses the gifts that God has given, it will be healthy and whole church.

To determine which gifts God has given you, it will involve the following considerations. First, seek God in prayer and ask Him to give you wisdom, understanding, and clarity to help you identify your spiritual gifts. God will be your greatest revealer. You can also take a spiritual gift assessment inventory. There are resources and suggested readings provided in the appendix of this book, and you may also have Christian friends or leaders who know you well and can help you identify your spiritual gifts. You will have to determine the best resource for you. Some of your gifts will be revealed to you by God as you voluntarily serve in the body of Christ.

TAKING A DEEPER DIVE

1) What natural abilities or talents do you possess?

   _____
   _____
   _____
   _____

2) What spiritual gift(s) has God given you?

   _____
   _____
   _____
   _____

3) Have you taken a spiritual gift assessment, and if so, what was your result?

   _____
   _____
   _____
   _____

4) Do you use your natural or spiritual gifts for the kingdom? Why or why not?

   _____
   _____
   _____
   _____

CHAPTER 5

FEEDING THE FLAME: RUNNING WITH GOD'S GIFTS

> *"Therefore, since we have so great a cloud of witnesses surrounding us, let us also lay aside every encumbrance and the sin which so easily entangles us, and let us run with endurance the race that is set before us, fixing our eyes on Jesus, the author and perfecter of faith...."*
> **(Hebrews 12:1-2 NASB 1995)**

There was a time at Rock church, where the church membership and the membership in the dance ministry were impacted due to a shift in leadership. During that time, there was only one dance ministry team remaining, the adult dance ministry, and that ministry was left with two members: me and another female. As time passed, I didn't feel led to rebuild the dance ministries from the ground up again. God had already been speaking to my heart letting me know that my time of leading LEAP Dance Ministry at Rock Church had come to an end. Yet, I did not want to step down without encouraging someone else who was equipped to take over the leadership of the ministry.

Through that experience, God showed me that stepping down from leadership did not mean that God had given up on me or that my service in my calling had cease. God still had more to show me, more to deposit in me, more for me to experience, and more for me to do as He takes me from glory to glory. Even when I thought my time of ministering in movement was over, God showed me otherwise. I was still being asked by my church and other people to choreograph a dance, teach a workshop, or minister in movement. I also continue to receive request to teach at one of EITI's TEN sites in Chicago. What God was saying to me is even though situations and circumstances can impact our lives, they do not control our calling. Despite what we see, experience, and feel, God can still use us, and often have more for us to do until He says otherwise. So, in learning that, I continue to allow God to use me as He gives me new assignments and as I embark on new callings in the ministry of movement.

Our gifts are to use while we are here on earth, and as God continues to open doors, it indicates that He still has more in store for us to do. Our responsibility is to continue to walk worthy of our calling, be a light to others, continue to grow in the area where God has planted us, and continue to seek His will. One day, when I was taking an aqua aerobics class, the instructor, in her jovial nature, said as she made direct eye contact with me, "Don't stop dancing." I never told the instructor I danced. Was this God speaking to me again as He spoke to me through the worship leader many years ago when He first called me to dance for Him? I would like to think so.

The fate of our calling is not for us to determine. God will let us know when we have completed our assignment, or when one season of our calling is over, and a new season has begun. In essence, God has the final say. If we are able and capable, God still wants to use us to be a light for others to see. God still wants to use us to mentor others with similar gifts, to build up more leaders, and to multiply His kingdom. We do not always need a title to validate our calling.

In general, when we use our gifts, we expand the mindset of the body of Christ. We impart understanding and purpose. For example, the ministry of movement has not always been accepted in the body of Christ, but as more people have been exposed to it and have sought biblical understanding of the gift, God has opened the hearts and minds of the churches. God has used the ministry of movement to praise and worship Him and proclaim His truths. The ministry of movement has also brought joy, deliverance, restoration, and encouragement to the body of Christ.

WALKING WORTHY OF YOUR CALLING

"So we keep on praying for you, asking our God to enable you to live a life worthy of his call. May he give you the power to accomplish all the good things your faith prompts you to do."

(2 Thessalonians 1:11 NLT)

Walk Worthy: Stay Committed

If we exercise the gifts, talents, and abilities that God has given us, God will give us more gifts, talents, and abilities. But if we try to hold on to them rather than using them for God's kingdom, they can become less effective over time. The enemy will take advantage of every opportunity that we give him to get us off track. He will infiltrate our hearts and minds with doubt, insecurities, pride, criticism, and judgment and give us reasons not to use the gifts, talents, and abilities God has given us. Consider Jesus' parable of the talents in Matthew 25:14-30: The men with the five and two talents used their talents, to gain double of what they had before, ten and four talents, respectively. But the man with the one talent hid his talent because he was afraid. That one talent was taken from the man and given to the man who now had ten talents.

The enemy wants to keep us in bondage so that we do not receive the blessings of God or cannot be a blessing to others. The enemy will whisper in our ears that we are not eloquent enough to speak before a group of people, or we do not have enough spiritual knowledge to teach that group, or someone other than us should lead the ministry. Remember that God has equipped us with everything we need to reach our destiny. We cannot allow people, temptations, trials, tribulations, and spiritual attacks to cause us not to use our gifts, talents, and abilities to fulfill our God-given purpose. We must remember the following: We are not working for man but for God. Joseph Prince writes, "We don't fight for victory; we fight from victory."[20] The Lord will fight our battles and provide whatever we need to complete any assignment that He has given us. We must persevere through all encounters of spiritual warfare, negative emotions, negative experiences, and negative feedback.

If we are committed to doing what God has called us to do, we will be content in our circumstances because even in our weaknesses, God will show Himself strong. If we are committed to doing what God calls us to do, we will allow God to position us and trust Him with the process. If we are committed to doing what God calls us to do, we will seek God and take advantage of every opportunity He provides. If we are committed to doing what God has called us to do, we will seek spiritual growth and development to perfect what He has given us. If we are committed to doing what God has called us to do, we will be willing to learn and glean from others. If we are committed to doing what God has called us to do, we will continue to move forward with a servant's attitude.

Walk Worthy: Seek God

Apart from God, we are nothing. God says this in John 15:5: *"I am the vine; you are the branches. If you remain in me and I in you, you will bear much fruit; apart from me you can do nothing"* (NIV). It is God who has done and is still doing everything for us.

So, what is one of the things God wants from us? God wants a relationship with us—a partnership where we can lean on Him and He can lead us in everything that He desires of us. God desires to supply all our needs. God desires to reveal to us His plans for our lives. God desires to reveal to us how to walk in our calling and use our gifts. God is such a gentleman that He does not force us to do anything. Our relationship with Him is based on trust and not force. It is a choice that we make because of our faith and love for Him.

Seeking God should bring us to a place of hearing God's voice. God often speaks to us in the quietness of our hearts reminding us of His love, strength, and power, and directing us in what He wants us to do and how He wants us to do it. There are times when we will need to be still or even silent so that we can have a listening ear and tune out every other voice but God. God can speak to us in multiple ways, including through scriptures, music, songs, praise, dance, dreams, nature, conversations with someone else, preaching, teaching, sickness, and our circumstances. Most importantly, God speaks to us through the Holy Spirit, moving in our thoughts, feelings, and senses.

God speaks to us and is ready to hear from us. He desires our songs of praise, our words of thanksgiving, and our words of adoration. He is ready to meet our every need according to His riches in glory in Christ Jesus. Everything we need to sustain us will be found when we commune with God.

Walk Worthy: Let Your Light Shine

> *"In the same way, let your light shine before others, so that they may see your good works and give glory to your Father who is in heaven."*
> **(Matthew 5:16 ESV)**

As Christians, God sees us and knows how we live before men. As God molds us into a new creation, there should be a difference in how we talk, act, and make choices for our lives. Other people should see qualities or characteristics in us that depict God at work in our lives. We are not trying to live for men or become someone we are not, because God wants us to be our authentic selves. We are letting go and allowing God to take the "will" of our lives. In fact, God will bring about the changes in our lives to glorify and honor Him. We cannot do it alone, because we will fail every attempt. For God to work in us, we must surrender.

For God to do His will in our lives, we must surrender our will. We must allow God to speak, direct, lead, teach, correct, and train in our lives to live His life. As stated in Romans 12:1-2, *"Therefore, I urge you, brothers, and sisters, given God's mercy, to offer your bodies as a living sacrifice, holy and pleasing to*

God—this is your true and proper worship. Do not conform to the pattern of this world but be transformed by the renewing of your mind. Then you will be able to test and approve what God's will is—his good, pleasing, and perfect will" (NIV).

As you give your entire being, your heart, love, talents, energy, and all your strength for God's service, God will mold your character, mature your faith, and transform your heart to become more like Him. As God changes your life, your identity in Christ will become more evident to others. People will then be able to affirm God's work in you and through you.

THE BLESSINGS OF GIFTS

> *"Eyes that focus on what is beautiful bring joy to the heart, and hearing a good report refreshes and strengthens the inner being."*
> **(Proverbs 15:30 TPT)**

God told Abraham that all nations of the earth would be blessed through him (Genesis 18:19). Do you realize how blessed we are? God has chosen, predestined, created, accepted, saved, and redeemed us through Jesus Christ. Through Jesus, God has made it possible for us to have a relationship with Him. He has given us purpose in His kingdom. He has given us grace, mercy, unconditional love, favor, and eternal life. We will spend eternity glorifying God, praising and worshipping, magnifying, and loving God. God has given us an inheritance, which is His kingdom, and all His promises and blessings. He has sealed us with His Holy Spirit to teach us, guide us, comfort us, and reveal to us.

Moreover, God heals and strengthens our bodies. He renews our minds. He gives us a heart of flesh instead of a heart of stone. We have been blessed with health, wholeness, soundness, prosperity, and every spiritual blessing. We are rich in Christ and lack no good thing. God has even given us the blessing of laughter so that we do not take life so seriously. Isn't it also a blessing to know that there is no condemnation for those in Christ Jesus? God is faithful to forgive us. God can turn our failures into successes. Romans 8:17 tells us that we are more than conquerors in Christ Jesus. We already have victory in every circumstance.

Knowing that God has blessed us with everything we need, we can confidently serve Him. We can rest in the fact that God will fulfill every promise He has made to us. We operate in God's grace and possess the victory to accomplish whatever He leads us to do. So, let us continue to run our course, allowing God to do the work He is doing in and through us.

FINISH THE RACE

"I have fought the good fight,
I have finished the race, I have kept the faith."
(2 Timothy 4:7 NIV)

A marathon race is a sport of confidence and willpower requiring training, endurance, and dedication. In a marathon, a runner is trained to pace himself because if he runs too fast, he will tire out, and if he runs too slow, he may give up. A marathon runner must be so in tune with his body that he knows how to maintain energy, patience, and drive throughout the entire race. More than anything else, a marathon runner must be disciplined enough to wake up early in the morning to run even during uncomfortable or inconvenient times, such as during rain or when experiencing bodily pain.

Living out our lives for Christ is like running a marathon race and not a sprint. We do not just run, but we run with God's gifts to help fulfill our purpose. This spiritual race requires faith, stamina, perseverance, commitment, and discipline. We need the discipline of prayer, studying God's Word, fellowshipping with other saints, praise and worship, evangelism, and service so we don't lose heart. Our responsibility is to be open with eyes to see, ears to hear, and the heart to receive what God is doing and how God is moving in our lives, and to walk into the season God has allowed us to be in. We must stay in alignment with the direction that God moves us in. The unexpected will happen such as shifts in ministry. We must allow God to shift us, shift the vision, shift the people, shift the place of ministry, or shift how we minister but, in the midst, we must continue to finish the race.

There may be times when people leave the ministry. Their calling or giftedness may not align with the ministry. They may fail to trust God or the ministry leader or God may be moving them on. Just because people leave ministries does not mean that the ministry is ending. Sometimes, God may be birthing something new and must remove the old to make way for the new. Isaiah 43:19 says, "Behold, I am going to do something new, now it will spring up; will you not be aware of it? I will even make a roadway in the wilderness, rivers in the desert" (NASB). We must be patient and wait on the Lord to see what God will do (Isaiah 40:31).

If we fix our eyes on Jesus, the author and perfecter of our faith (Hebrews 12:2), we will never be disappointed. The Amplified Bible defines "fixing our eyes" as "looking away from all that will distract us." Looking to Jesus tells me that we turn to Him for all our needs, expecting Him to help and rescue us. We must fix our spiritual eyes and tune our spiritual ears to what God is showing us. The Amplified Bible also tells us that Jesus being the "author and perfecter of faith" means that He is "the first incentive for our belief and the One who brings our faith to maturity." Jesus has already reached the finish line and is now at the right hand of God, interceding for us so that we may accomplish what God has predestined for us to do. Jesus understands suffering, has been tempted in every way possible yet without sin, and can sympathize with our weakness. It is Jesus who we should draw near to and who can help us in our time of need.

If we persevere in our God-given purpose, God will use our gifts and bless our lives. God's plan is always designed to bring Him glory while serving His people. Serving in any capacity is not always easy, but God will give us the strength to thrive in our giftedness and to be overcomers. No matter the situation or circumstance, we must believe that God can do the impossible, and we must stay in the race running with our gifts and never give up on ourselves, God, or His calling on our lives.

When a runner finishes a marathon race, they normally receive medals, ribbons, and certificates of completion. As we fulfill God's purpose in our lives, we will obtain rewards that goes beyond the tangible. One of our rewards will encompass the pleasure of serving and seeing God do the work in the people we serve. It is rewarding just to see people come to know the Lord, grow in their faith, and start to use their gifts. God will reward us with power, strength, knowledge, faith, peace, wisdom, insight, inexpressible joy, and every heavenly treasure to function within the capacity to which He has called us.

One day, we will eventually spend eternity with our Heavenly Father, who promises to reward us for a job well done. When God accepts us in His loving arms, we will be able to hear Him say, *"Well done, good and faithful servant! You have been faithful with a few things; I will put you in charge of many things. Come and share your master's happiness!"* (Matthew 25:21 NIV).

TAKING A DEEPER DIVE

1) What helps you stay committed to your calling, ministry, or service?

   _____

   _____

   _____

   _____

2) In what ways have you felt blessed by using your gifts?

   _____

   _____

   _____

   _____

3) What do you need to do, or what are you doing, where God can say, "Well done, good and faithful servant!"?

   _____

   _____

   _____

   _____

A FINAL WORD

*"But you shall be called the priests of the Lord;
they shall speak of you as the ministers of our God."*
(Isaiah 61:6 ESV)

In this book, I have shared the journey that God took me on to help build my faith and trust in Him by walking in my purpose and utilizing the gifts He has given me. Because I aligned my will with His will for my life, I experienced firsthand what God can do and how God can work in and through us out of His love for us. Your journey, calling, and gifts may differ from mine, but at the end of the day, it is all about saving souls and changing lives for the cause of Christ. Salvation is impossible without knowledge of the gospel or the righteousness of God, which can only be shared or displayed by God's children who exercise their gifts.

Romans 10:14-15 states it this way: *"How then will they call on him in whom they have not believed? And how are they to* believe in him of whom they have never heard? And how are they to hear without someone preaching? And how are they to preach unless they are sent? As it is written, 'How beautiful are the feet of those who preach the good news!'"* (NIV). We have the beautiful feet that God is calling on to impact the world today.

The gifts assist us in conducting God's Great Commission. God calls us and then sends us out to different platforms to save, deliver, heal, comfort, give hope, and proclaim God. We do not necessarily have to look for our purpose but to walk into it through our relationship with God. God has equipped us with gifts to work in partnership with Him. In fact, God's gifts will carry us from glory to glory in Him. We possess natural gifts, the fruit of the Spirit, and spiritual gifts for God's glory and to help us fulfill our purpose. Natural gifts such as singing, dancing, and speaking are abilities and talents that God has given us. Fruit of the Spirit, such as love, joy, and peace, are the attributes that the Holy Spirit produces in us to help us develop Christ-like character. Spiritual gifts such as prophecy, speaking in tongues, and the gift of healing are individually given to believers through the Holy Spirit according to God's choosing so that the church can be whole, unified, strengthened, and encouraged, growing together as the body of Christ.

In Galatians 6:9-10, Paul reminds us, *"Let us not become weary in doing good, for at the proper time we will reap a harvest if we do not give up. Therefore, as we have opportunity, let us do good to all people, especially to those who belong to*

A Final Word

the family of believers" (NIV). Every good and perfect gift that God has bestowed upon us will enable us to do good works and shine as lights in a dark world. As God leads us, let us be movers, shakers, and life changers. May we have the eyes to see, the ears to hear, and the heart to seek, to find, to become, and to do all that God has planned for our lives.

APPENDIX

SUGGESTED READING AND RESOURCES

1) Arthur, Kay, David Lawson, and BJ Lawson. 2010. *Understanding Spiritual Gifts*.

2) Davis, Shirley Giles. 2018. *God. Gifts. You.* (six-week Bible study).

3) Online Spiritual Gift Assessment. https://www.livingwatercoast.com/thegifts?gad_source=1&gclid=EAIaIQobChMIooCD9_y_hAMV3_dMAh0U4QpKEAAYBCAAEgJ8yPD_BwE.

4) Wagner, C. Peter. 2003. *Finding Your Spiritual Gifts* (self-guided questionnaire).

DESCRIPTION OF SPIRITUAL GIFTS

"Spiritual gifts are special abilities, talents, or capacities given to individual Christians by the Holy Spirit for the purpose of serving God and others within the Christian community. These gifts are not natural talents or skills but supernatural endowments provided by God's grace. They are meant to be used to build up the body of Christ, which is the community of believers."[21]

1) Apostle – One sent forth with a specific commission to establish and build the church.

2) Prophet – An individual who receives divine revelations and communicate God's message.

3) Evangelist – One who proclaims the gospel and lead others to faith in Christ.

4) Pastor (Shepherd); One who provides spiritual care and guidance to the church.

5) Teacher – One who is skilled in explaining and sharing god's Word.

6) Wisdom A deep understanding of god's truth and the ability to apply it practically to life situations.

7) Workers of Miracles – Believers who perform extraordinary signs and wonders.

Appendix

8) Knowledge – Special insight and knowledge of God's Word and His will.

9) Faith – A supernatural ability to trust God and His promises in extraordinary circumstances.

10) Gifts of Healing – Those with the gift of praying for and witnessing healing.

11) Miracles – The ability to perform extraordinary signs and wonders, demonstrating God's power.

12) Prophecy – Speaking forth God's messages, including words of edification, exhortation, and comfort.

13) Discernment of Spirits – Distinguishing between different spirits, discerning whether they are of God, human, or evil origin.

14) Speaking in Tongues – The ability to speak in an unknown language as a form of prayer or communication with God.

15) Interpretation of Tongues – The gift of interpreting messages in tongues, making them understandable to others.

16) Serving – The capacity to serve others selflessly and meet practical needs within the church.

17) Teaching – The ability to communicate and explain god's truth effectively to others.

18) Encouragement – The gift of encouraging and motivating others toward spiritual growth and maturity.

19) Giving – The ability to give generously and cheerfully, often contributing resources for the benefit of the church and those in need.

20) Leadership – The gift of providing leadership, organization, and guidance within the church.

21) Mercy – The gift of showing compassion, empathy, and kindness to those who are suffering or in distress.

22) Helpers– Individuals who serve others selflessly, often behind the scenes.

23) Administration (Leadership) – Those who provide guidance and organization within the church.[22]

ENDNOTES

1. Donald Lawrence and the Tri-City Singers.

2. "Surrender (religion)," Wikipedia, https://en.wikipedia.org/wiki/Surrender_(religion).

3. Rick Warren, *The Purpose Driven Life* (Zondervan, 2002).

4. "What Does 1 John 2:5 Mean?," Knowing Jesus, https://dailyverse.knowing-jesus.com/1-john-2-5.

5. "Declaring Faith: What It Means to Proclaim in the Bible," Biblifocus, October 22, 2023, https://biblifocus.com/blog/what-does-it-mean-in-the-bible-to-proclaim/.

6. Janet Denison, "What Is Your Kingdom Purpose?," https://www.foundationswithjanet.org/columns/blog-columns/what-is-your-kingdom-purpose/.

7. "Identity," *Psychology Today*, https://www.psychologytoday.com/us/basics/identity.

8. Joseph Prince, *Destined to Reign Devotional* (2008).

9. Valerie Murray, "Why Does God Give Christians the Gift of the Holy Spirit?," September 20, 2019, https://valeriemurray.com/why-does-god-give-christians-the-gift-of-the-holy-spirit/.

10 "What is the Key to Bearing Fruit as a Christian?," Got Questions, https://www.gotquestions.org/bearing-fruit.html.

11 Danielle Bernock (Contributing Writer), "What are Spiritual Gifts? Definitions., Types, and Examples," January 18, 2024, https://www.christianity.com/wiki/christian-life/what-are-spiritual-gifts-understanding-the-types-and-discovering-yours.html.

12 Shirley Davis, *God.Gifts.You.*, Calling Video.

13 Kay Arthur, David Lawson, and BJ Lawson, *Understanding Spiritual Gifts* (Precept Ministries International, 2010).

14 Danielle Bernock (Contributing Writer), "What are Spiritual Gifts? Definitions., Types, and Examples."

15 Kay Arthur, David Lawson, and BJ Lawson, Understanding Spiritual Gifts (Precept Ministries International, 2010).

16 Danielle Bernock (Contributing Writer), "What are Spiritual Gifts? Definitions., Types, and Example."

17 "Manifestation Gifts." Neue Thing, https://neuething.org/manifestation-gifts/#:~:text=The%20manifestation%20gifts%20are%20%E2%80%9Csupernatural,discerning%20spirits%2C%20speaking%20in%20tongues.

18 Danielle Bernock (Contributing Writer), "What are Spiritual Gifts? Definitions., Types, and Examples."

19 Danielle Bernock (Contributing Writer), "What are Spiritual Gifts? Definitions., Types, and Examples."

20 Joseph Prince, *Destined to Reign Devotional* (2008).

21 Danielle Bernock (Contributing Writer), "What are Spiritual Gifts? Definitions., Types, and Example."

22 Danielle Bernock (Contributing Writer), "What are Spiritual Gifts? Definitions., Types, and Example."

www.ingramcontent.com/pod-product-compliance
Lightning Source LLC
Chambersburg PA
CBHW071739090426
42738CB00011B/2527